HAUS CURIOSITIES

The UK's In-Out Referendum

About the Author

David Owen (Lord Owen) trained as a medical doctor and practised as a neurologist before being elected a Labour MP in his home city of Plymouth. He served as Foreign Secretary under James Callaghan from 1977 until 1979, and later co-founded and went on to lead the Social Democratic Party (SDP). Between 1992–95 Lord Owen served as EU peace negotiator in the former Yugoslavia, and he now sits as an Independent Social Democrat in the House of Lords. He is the author of many books, including *In Sickness and In Power, The Hubris Syndrome* and *The Hidden Perspective*.

David Owen

THE UK'S IN-OUT REFERENDUM

EU Foreign and Defence Policy Reform

HAUS
CURIOSITIES

First published by Haus Publishing in 2015
70 Cadogan Place
London SW1X 9AH
www.hauspublishing.com

The right of the author to be identified as the author
of this work has been asserted in accordance with
the Copyright, Designs and Patents Act 1988

A CIP catalogue record for this book is
available from the British Library

Print ISBN: 978-1-910376-53-9
Ebook ISBN: 978-1-910376-54-6

Typeset in Garamond by MacGuru Ltd
info@macguru.org.uk

Printed in Spain

The UK's In-Out Referendum

There is a grave danger that the European Union will go on pretending, despite the UK negotiation, that it can avoid or delay making the structural changes that it urgently needs to convince the people in its Member States that it can overcome the formidable problems it now faces. Six years on, the Eurozone is still in the midst of an economic crisis. Greece's problems are not resolved. The French and Italian economies are still not confronting their need for radical change and there are serious weaknesses in other Eurozone economies. Geopolitically, the EU's pursuit of conflict resolution leaves much to be desired. The EU policy over its Association Agreement with the Ukraine triggered the conflict in that country and there are now serious related military tensions developing on the Russian Federation's borders with the three Baltic states, Estonia, Latvia and Lithuania, to which NATO is responding. There is trouble brewing in Bosnia-Herzegovina where the behaviour of the Bosnian Serbs shows few signs of being checked by Serbia. Public tolerance is stretched by uncontrolled economic migration into the EU from Syria and other countries, like Eritrea and even Afghanistan. The so-called Islamic State is now occupying Iraq and Syria, has attacked Beirut in Lebanon and a Russian plane over Egypt, and operates from Darnah in Libya. The EU has yet to agree a coherent policy towards Turkey. Its policy of 'common defence' within the European Common Security and Defence Policy[1], CSDP, risks deeply damaging competition with NATO planning and its cohesion.

This booklet is about how the foreign and defence policies of the EU and the geopolitical problems of the wider Europe are inextricably linked to the negotiations prior to the UK voting on whether to remain in or leave the EU. That vote will have to take place by the end of 2017, though it looks as if the government will try and rush it through in the summer of 2016. If the EU dismisses this period of negotiation as one of little significance to them and as a matter just for the British, it will sleepwalk into a catastrophe. The outcome will have profound economic and geopolitical consequences, not just for those parts covered by the EU and NATO, but for the whole of wider Europe (*see diagram on page 3*).

When an ever more integrated Eurozone emerges and starts to vote *en bloc* within the EU, it will be vital for a Non-Eurozone qualified majority to have been established and to be able to prevent Eurozone domination in not just the Single Market but in all aspects of the EU, particularly foreign and security policy. The extent to which the Eurozone moves to give more authority to voting in the Eurozone bodies and the European Parliament depends on how ready Eurozone Member States are to mirror the democratic procedures of a single country, give up unanimity, rely more on a simple majority or increase the number of Member States needed to form a blocking minority – all steps towards a United States of Europe. If the Eurozone deals with its democratic deficit through democratic enhancement, then it is essential to establish the right for a Non-Eurozone Member State to

A Restructured Europe

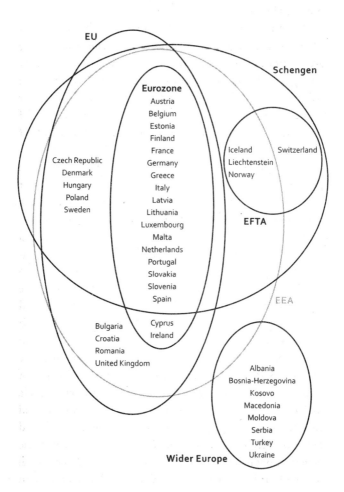

block or opt-out of changes to the architecture of not just the Single Market but also EU foreign and defence policies and, if need be, revert to the consensus of European Community Political Cooperation for foreign and security policies.

Amending the treaties' language is being refused in advance of France and Germany holding their elections in 2017. But since the Maastricht Treaty was written assuming that all EU countries would inexorably join the Eurozone, which they are clearly not doing, why can't this change be made by unanimity in the European Council? That mechanism was part of the Lisbon Treaty. The cardinal sin of the EU was in abandoning the supranational and the intergovernmental pillared structure that was part of the Maastricht Treaty compromise. Eurozone integration will not establish a consensus decision-making body but one where the majority gets its way; inevitably this will overflow into foreign and defence decision-making unless new powers to check this are built into the treaties.

Ever greater political integration is the fundamental issue behind and within the UK demand for a major renegotiation and a referendum. It is why the government has singled out the wording 'ever closer union'. Though it applies to the peoples and not to the nations in the treaties, a formulation accepted even by Margaret Thatcher, it has come through persistent application of what is called the Community Method to mean nations. It was these words 'ever closer union' that David Cameron strongly objected to and was the reason for his party withdrawing from the Christian Democratic grouping in the European Parliament, deeply resented by Angela Merkel. To change that interpretation requires more than a statement – it needs treaty change too. Not surprisingly, those who have already started today to campaign for the UK to remain in the EU are often people who have supported Eurozone membership for the UK on every past occasion it has been open to debate. Many of them still passionately wish to maintain the option of Eurozone membership for the future. Many also resisted the European Act 2011 that triggers a referendum in the UK before any further loss of British sovereignty can be conceded by ministers. This Act was William Hague's achievement when Foreign Secretary, along with EU recognition that foreign policy decisions have to also be described as Member States' decisions to be legally approved. But the Act alone is not enough. We cannot have referenda on every issue and yet ever greater unity is built up on the basis of many small decisions not least by the European Court of Justice (ECJ).

US politicians and officials should be much franker when commenting on whether the UK should remain in or leave the EU. It took centuries to develop a single currency across the USA and that country, moreover, had from its foundation chosen to have a single language. We are dealing with very sensitive issues of national identity and human instinct in the EU the more it develops. It should surprise no one, given public resistance to ever closer union in many countries, that we have already adopted a union of different speeds; there are manifest signs that the pace of integration chosen by the Commission in Brussels is all too frequently either too fast or wrongly designed for people in some Member States. The test for European political leaders now is: how sensitive can they become to the realities of the need for treaty amendment? On this there are few grounds for optimism; too often the

European institutions are resistant to treaty change. Restructuring is not about a two-speed Europe, but a Europe of many different speeds reinforced by treaty change with which the ECJ have to reckon.

The newly appointed chief economist to the IMF, Maurice Obstfeld, previously an adviser to President Obama, has been outspoken on the 'trilemma' the Eurozone faces, namely that it cannot pursue cross-border financial integration and maintain stability while protecting national fiscal independence. He is very clear: 'Parallel moves towards political union are an essential complement in ensuring that national electorates accept the legitimacy of decisions made in the common interest.' The problem in the EU now is that more and more national electorates are increasingly not accepting that transferring money from their country to another is in the common good on such a wide scale as envisaged by some in the Eurozone. The resistance over transferring to Greece did not just come up against public opinion in Germany; it was a vocal issue in Finland, Lithuania and Slovenia as well as the Netherlands and Belgium.

A restructured European Single Market is not a massive task. The EU's variable geometry has been evolving ever since the Maastricht Treaty negotiations on the euro ended in December 1990. As I argue in the ebook version of *Europe Restructured. The Eurozone Crisis and the UK Referendum*[2], restructuring the EU necessitates two distinct elements: a Eurozone grouping and a Non-Eurozone grouping, both together within the Single Market of the existing European Economic Area (EEA) which comprises all EU Member States plus Norway, Iceland and Liechtenstein. These three countries at present are not full voting members, but this should change along with all new members being given full voting rights under qualified majority voting (QMV).

A wider Europe membership of the EEA should also be offered, starting with invitations to Switzerland and Turkey, the latter already an associate EU member. It would involve all the advantages and obligations of full EEA membership except that such countries would not be automatically offered the freedom of movement within the EU of people and labour. This is not a necessity for the effective working of a Single Market, but it is essential for membership of a more integrated Eurozone. EU countries like the UK that have no intention of joining the Eurozone and already control their own borders, not being part of the Schengen open border grouping within the EU, would be able to opt-out from free movement of people and labour from any *new* Member State. This is a better route forward than trying to retrospectively withhold the right to claim benefits for a period of years within the UK by citizens of EU states like Poland, Bulgaria and Romania. It will do very little to reduce the numbers coming to the UK and it is numbers that are at the heart of public debate – numbers that have been regularly underestimated by successive UK governments. This debate has been heightened by Chancellor Merkel's promise to Turkey to speed up EU entry with free movement of people. That promise, she knows, is vehemently opposed by some Member States, particularly France. Failing to fulfil this opportunistic promise will make it harder to achieve an urgently needed EU-Turkish accord, which can come in 2016 through Turkish membership of the EEA.

The UK referendum on the EU must be conducted with scrupulous fairness and must not be open to manipulation, otherwise referendums will be seen even more as a device for achieving governmental policy through bypassing parliament and democracy. This is not just a perception. Referendums involve a reduction in the independent judgement of parliamentarians through their acceptance of a structure that, though technically advisory, in effect, compels them to enact the result in legislation, regardless of how they themselves voted. Correctly applied referendums can enhance parliamentary democracy. But we must recognise that there are different types of referendum and different reasons for calling them. The Scottish referendum was about separating from the UK. The In-Out EU referendum is about the UK remaining in or leaving the EU. Obvious to state, but necessary to remind people this referendum is not a vehicle for Scotland to separate from the UK. The Scottish people rejected that choice in 2014. The agreement of the whole of the UK for a re-run of the Scottish referendum will not be given again for some time and certainly not in the near future whenever the Scottish government think they can win.

Pretension is the besetting sin of the institutions that have throughout the last fifty years grown up to protect the present EU, whether from the creation of what was initially called the European Economic Community (EEC) in 1957, also known as the Common Market, to the European Community in 1967, and since 1993 the European Union.

The emergence of the Single Market was a formidable achievement until it was foolishly endangered by the flawed design and failing operation of the Eurozone from 1990. The

Single European Act of 1986 which brought it about was supported by all the political parties then represented in the House of Commons and there is still today very little party political controversy about the working arrangements of the Single Market. Yet there are signs of corporate sclerosis settled comfortably within its framework and the scandal over the Volkswagen diesel emission story is a warning that all is not well. The Dutch and German Finance Ministers are right to put reform and restructuring of the Single Market high on their agenda for 2016 during the Dutch Presidency and they know treaty amendment is inevitable.

If the only option in the forthcoming UK referendum becomes a minimalist renegotiation – in effect, window dressing and a disguised status quo – there is a real chance that the British people will, and in my view should, vote to leave the EU, adopting what is called in shorthand terms Brexit. But it is dangerous to choose this course unless it is accompanied by a new national spirit of endeavour built on realism, a recognition that we are taking a rigorous not a relaxed choice, that we are embarking on a global mission and will no longer be cushioned within Europe. We have not resolved our own economic problems yet and there are difficulties ahead of us, but it is a fact of which we can be proud that the UK has met its UN and NATO targets – spending 0.7 per cent of our national income on foreign aid and 2 per cent on defence. To pretend that this country is too weak politically, economically and militarily to vote to leave the EU is absurd and deserves to be laughed out of court.

The evolution of the EU did not start in 1957 with the six founding Member States of the EEC negotiating in

Messina. Nor did that make the major contribution to peace in Europe. That process started in terms of *realpolitik* even before the end of the Second World War when Winston Churchill visited Joseph Stalin in Moscow on 9 October 1944. It resulted in two spheres of post-war influence emerging over Europe, with the USSR on one side and the US and UK on the other. On a half-sheet of paper which was passed between the two men Greece was placed in the UK's sphere of influence and, in return, with Stalin's big tick across the wording, Romania was placed under the USSR's influence. The fact that Romania is now in the EU is a salutary lesson as viewed from Putin's Kremlin of how Russia's influence has diminished at the expense of the EU's enlargement.

Spheres of influence may not disappear – they can fade, but then reopen. The conflict in Ukraine starting in 2014 has deep roots reflecting spheres of influence over the centuries. When Roosevelt, Churchill and Stalin met in Tehran in 1943, then at Yalta in February 1945 and finally at the Potsdam Conference in August the same year, spheres of influence featured large. Even so, by early 1946 it looked as if the US would draw back across the Atlantic. Had that happened Western Europe and the USSR would have faced each other, both economically weak but with Stalin still possessing a mighty war machine in the East that had played the critical part in outright victory over Hitler's forces.

It is salutary, given the current focus on Greece in Europe, to note that in 1946 the very future of Greece as a viable nation was at risk. At six weeks' notice the US took over the financial burden of supporting Greece from a UK driven to relinquish its leading role by financial constraints. The Truman Doctrine was thereby established and the President decided that the US would not withdraw militarily from Europe and would use its economic, and if need be military, power to prevent further European countries coming under Soviet influence, starting with Greece. Some in Europe today want the US to abandon Europe as one of their chosen spheres of influence. To which I say be careful what you wish for.

The US fortunately followed the Truman Doctrine with a new policy stemming from George Marshall's speech at Harvard University on 5 June 1947. It was Ernest Bevin, the British Foreign Secretary, who turned the words of the former general, by then American Secretary of State, into what he called 'a lifeline to sinking men' which 'seemed to bring hope where there was none'. Marshall, Roosevelt's former military commander, had learnt the fundamental lesson of the Paris Peace Conference of January–July 1919 and was determined that there should be no punitive peace enforced on Germany. He initiated a process called Marshall aid that pumped $13 billion, the equivalent today of more than $150 billion, into Europe over four years. It was Marshall aid more than any other single political act that made possible today's European Union. Britain was the single biggest beneficiary with 26 per cent of the total. France received 18 per cent and West Germany 11 per cent; Greece took less than 3 per cent, though that sum represented 200 per cent of its national output.

The Americans did understand the need to save Greece in 2015, and the importance of generous debt relief for the post-war German economy; the Obama Administration has pressed and still presses for a debt write-off for Greece. What some in the Obama Administration, and in particular the

US State Department, do not admit is that the present European Union is on an escalator towards political integration in all aspects of EU policies, inevitably extending into foreign policy and defence. For some this allows the US to focus on China and slowly withdraw from Europe.

US foreign policy experts should ask themselves, with more realism than hitherto, whether a fully integrated EU defence and foreign policy in the actual circumstances of our time – Putin's Russia, Xi's China – is in America's interests. It used to be a rational assumption that the EU strengthened NATO, but the reality is that this is no longer a safe supposition. Nor can the US rely on the UK ensuring NATO's interests are upheld within the EU unless the UK negotiates different treaty language. Today, in the context of greater integration forced on the EU by Eurozone failure, unless a renegotiation allows the UK to escape from ever more qualified voting on foreign and defence policy, there will be profound consequences for UK and US interests. The continued coherence and strength of NATO in some circumstances could be better served by UK withdrawal from any CSDP and even CFSP dominated by an increasingly integrated Eurozone. Yet why is that argument not even being heard within the referendum debate? The reason is that David Cameron's campaign links continued EU membership to 'national security' – saying Europe has 'stood up to Russia' – but fails to mention that the stiffening for this comes from Washington. His campaign points out that the EU helped to stop Iran's nuclear programme. True, but it was Obama who gave this policy personal priority and worked with Russia as well as the three EU countries who started the dialogue. Cameron even invokes the EU stopping Somali piracy. One is bound to ask whether Cameron has forgotten about Libya.

The assessment of the former British Chief of Defence Staff, General David Richards, in his book *Taking Command*[3] was from the start that though Obama was reluctant, 'any military campaign in Libya had to be a NATO operation. Some around [David Cameron] were quite attracted to the idea of it being an essentially Anglo-French operation – something President Sarkozy was advocating – but we could not have done it with the French alone. We needed the Americans alongside us, particularly in the critical area of command and control and surveillance/intelligence, and for NATO to take responsibility.' Besides noting that an aircraft carrier would have made life a lot easier, he noted we had underestimated the incoherence, even anarchy, of the tribal and militia patch-work that filled the vacuum left by the Gaddafi regime.

The Libyan 'no-fly-zone' intervention starting in March 2011, which I also supported, was called for by the Arab League and backed by the UK and France with initially only a leading role for the US. It turned out an abysmal failure. In part this was because Russia and China, having reluctantly decided to abstain in the Security Council, then found themselves aligned by default with the destruction of all Gaddafi's ground-to-air missiles followed by regime change. It was foolish for the US, UK and France not to call together the Russian/NATO Council to explain why Gaddafi could not be ring-fenced to survive as leader when he fought to maintain total control. Robert Gates, who was President Bush's Secretary for Defense from 2006 and then went on to serve under President Obama, gave a farewell speech to NATO at its Headquarters in Brussels in June 2011, which I think Cameron should re-read. It said, 'The mightiest military alliance in history is only 11 weeks into an operation against a poorly armed regime in a sparsely populated country, yet many allies are beginning to run short of munitions, requiring the US, once more, to make up the difference ....We have the spectacle of an air operations center [in Italy] designed to handle more than 300 sorties a day struggling to launch about 150.' Gates was telling it straight to a Europe that had gotten so used to pretending it had adequate military capabilities that though 'all NATO members voted for the Libya mission less than half participated in the strike mission ... [with] many of the allies sitting on the sidelines ... not because they do not want to participate, but simply because they can't. The military capabilities simply aren't there.' Reiterating that the US share of NATO military spending had soared to 75 per cent Gates said very simply and poignantly, 'The US public will not stand for this much longer.'

The 28 Member States of the EU and their institutions must rethink and work together to restructure the whole EU, not just its parts. There are fundamental questions that have been evaded within the EU since the creation of the euro in 1990. The Maastricht Treaty was flawed, known to be flawed, and must now to be amended. Any EU restructuring, with or without the emergence of a more integrated Eurozone grouping, has to create a less integrated Non-Eurozone grouping, with both groupings in the Single Market under the EEA Treaty. The relationship between CSDP and NATO has to be rebooted.

The European Central Bank (ECB) is not a normal central bank because it is the central bank of a half-baked currency union. Were the ECB a normal central bank, when Greece was facing a run on its banks it would have lent, and if it thought Greek banks insolvent it would have had to recapitalise them and fund them through a properly constructed European stability mechanism. The fact that it has been inhibited from doing so at every turn in the Greek crisis is a reflection of the flawed nature of the legislation covering European Monetary Union (EMU). Reform of the ECB goes hand in hand with the as yet unanswered question about whether Germany, the Netherlands, Belgium and Finland – the prominent agnostics – are ready to integrate further and develop the whole Eurozone as a transfer union, where financial resources move from richer regions and countries to poorer ones, or to accept a much smaller Eurozone. But that issue also needs to be answered by the poorer regions and countries hanging on in the Eurozone. Are they ready to accept the disciplines associated with a transfer union, though not necessarily to the extent which Germany exacted on Greece? This question is all too often avoided by Italy and France and is now being challenged by the new government in Portugal and may also be raised in Spain and even Greece.

In 2016 the EU will face complex arguments about austerity that will dominate in the parliaments of all the Member States. Whether one agrees or disagrees with German attitudes to austerity, the open letter in 2015 to Angela Merkel from Heiner Flassbeck, former State Secretary in the German Federal Ministry of Finance, Thomas Piketty of the Paris School of Economics, Jeffrey D. Sachs of Columbia University, Dani Rodrik of Harvard Kennedy School and Simon Wren-Lewis of the University of Oxford represents the views of a significant section of opinion, left and right, on the global economic spectrum. They argue that the

> financial demands made by Europe have crushed the Greek economy, led to mass unemployment, a collapse of the banking system, made the external debt crisis far worse, with the debt problem escalating to an unpay-able 175 per cent of GDP. The economy now lies broken with tax receipts nose-diving, output and employment depressed, and businesses starved of capital. The humani-tarian impact has been colossal – 40 per cent of children now live in poverty, infant mortality is now sky rocketing and youth unemployment is close to 50 per cent ...

Restructuring the European treaties is not a matter for continued high-profile, bilateral meetings in Paris or Berlin. Whether they like it or not, Angela Merkel and François Hollande must also involve David Cameron and all 25 other heads of government at a formative stage. I do not believe the UK is coming to this renegotiation from a selfish British standpoint, nor that we and we alone have all the answers. The British negotiation position must be neither seen nor presented as narrow or self-seeking; we are all Europeans, but diverse and distinct. A flexible and viable new design is inevitable as we learn from the obvious mistakes of the exist-ing design. Sometimes in the EU waiting like Mr Micawber for 'something to turn up' is a viable strategy, but this UK referendum is a wake-up call, and one that we dare not sleep through in the light of the conflict in the Ukraine and Syria and could develop again in the Balkans. The bomb that brought down the Russian tourist plane flying out of Sharm-el-Sheik for which ISIL is responsible is a grim warning of worse to come, very likely from Africa and Asia.

Grievous errors have been made in the speed of EU expansion, particularly in how fast we went from 15 to 28 members. The political decision to bolster Greece's new democracy after the collapse of the Greek military junta in 1974 was a good one. When I chaired the European Council of Foreign Ministers weekend meeting at Leeds Castle in the spring of 1977 and Greek entry to the European Community was in principle agreed, we were unashamedly making a political choice to buttress their return to democracy after military rule. We also discussed Spain and Portugal, both of which had become democracies after the long dictatorships of Franco and Salazar. Eventually President Giscard d'Estaing, Chancellor Schmidt and Prime Minister Callaghan agreed on the timing, deciding that Greece would come in first – the French President having committed himself to the new Prime Minister Karamanlis. But Giscard d'Estaing also pledged to not postpone or object to the date fixed for the other two. Greece has had the most difficulty of these three countries with the transition, particularly after joining the Eurozone, having lied and rigged their economic data.

Undoubtedly pretending that no country could ever leave the Eurozone led the European Commission, at one stage, to warn Greece publicly it would have to leave the EU if it did so. The basis of such a law never existed. Upholding a non-existent law was but one of the most distasteful aspects of the bullying of Greece. First Prime Minister Papandreou was told by Angela Merkel and Nicolas Sarkozy he could not call a referendum and he relented; then Prime Minister Tsipras was also warned against calling a referendum, which fortunately he ignored.

The unresolved problems for the EU in relation to Ukraine are formidable. Ukraine is another country to suffer from EU pretension, in this case over its CFSP. It was surely not beyond the capacity of the EU External Affairs Secretariat to warn their boss, the High Representative, that the Commission in drawing up the Association Agreement with Ukraine risked a serious confrontation with Russia. Did they not recognise that the Putin who returned as President of the Russian Federation in May 2012, after his initial two terms and following the presidency of Medvedev, was bound to be a very different political leader? Was it not obvious that he was poised to make his presence felt across the wider Europe in the light of the policies he had developed during the five-day Russo-Georgian War of August 2008? Shortly after Georgia, Russian armed forces had already been set on a path of reform and re-equipment and trained to infiltrate. Putin himself had clearly vowed that never again was he going to be treated with a superficial friendliness by a US President, as when George W. Bush said he had 'looked the man in the eye'. We in the West often forget that Putin had made an unprecedented offer of friendship to Bush and the United States immediately after 9/11, reinforcing his offer with concrete measures and the unilateral announcement of the closure of bases in Cuba and North Korea.

Russia, by 2012, as Putin saw it, was a BRIC country rich in oil, gas and minerals, confident that it was a rising power and determined to figure on the world stage, along with

Brazil, India and China. Putin's generation of KGB officers had been, for the most part, cautious, pragmatic, Andropov-like reformers, and now they had watched with apprehension the march of liberal democracy and market reforms spreading rapidly through EU expansion. From May 2004 Poland, Hungary, the Czech Republic, Slovakia and Slovenia – the last mentioned formerly part of Tito's Yugoslavia – had come into the EU, as had the three Baltic states, Estonia, Latvia and Lithuania, a particular problem for Russia.

The old USSR believed that after the signing of the Helsinki Final Act of 1975, as Andrei Gromyko had argued with me in Moscow in 1977, the Western democracies had accepted the annexation of the Baltic states, undertaken by Stalin in 1942. After Boris Yeltsin that view reappeared. Then in the Mediterranean, Cyprus and Malta had also joined the EU and the Russian Federation became more attached to Syria where they had had a naval base since 1971. In 2007 there was a further expansion of the EU to include Bulgaria and Romania, in part a reward for refusing the rights of Russian planes to overfly their countries at the time of the Kosovo War in 1990. Putin, however, despite all this still did not give up even when rebuffed by President George W. Bush, and when Barack Obama came into office Putin was still calling for a greater Europe from Lisbon to Vladivostok and even offered the US a strategic partnership in a speech in Berlin in 2010. Then in 2013 Croatia joined the EU, but not Bosnia-Herzegovina.

With EU enlargement came NATO enlargement in 1999 and West European political and military structures took over very significant areas of territory that used to be under Soviet control. Ukraine wanted to join those structures demonstrably under the Orange Revolution of 2004 and again in 2013. Russians saw this as a provocation and was ready to resist.[4]

The ins and outs of what private pressure was fed into the EU's CFSP team in Brussels and by who – whether the Poles, the Germans, the CIA and/or the US State Department – to push to include security issues in such detail over Ukraine is not yet clear. Nor do we know the full extent of exactly what the then Polish Foreign Minister, Radosław Sikorski, was advocating in the negotiations on behalf of the EU. It is possible, however, to make a relatively well-informed guess. Certainly everything went badly wrong politically between the Ukraine and the EU well before Putin responded militarily. There has been an understandable reluctance to probe fully the Brussels side of the negotiations in the early stages of the Ukraine fighting to find out how the European Commission and the external affairs machinery together came up with the exact wording of the Association Agreement. But this must not be allowed to continue. There needs to be an honest retrospective analysis. For some in Brussels the Agreement was seen as another 'hour of Europe'. A Bosnian moment, a chance for the EU, not NATO, to lead in Europe. This type of competition was very dangerous then and is even more so today when we need both the EU and NATO acting in harmony, not competition.

The Association Agreement was meant to have been signed at the Vilnius summit of the Eastern Partnership in late November 2013. What soon became apparent when the wording of the Agreement began to leak out was that very few senior EU politicians in their capitals had even bothered to read the detailed wording. No political alarm bells apparently rang. The Commission document went through in Brussels. In London nothing stirred. A political problem with the Ukraine and Russia should have been flagged up in the Foreign Office much earlier. The words in the draft Association Agreement were, by any standard, inflammatory for any recent Russian leaders – not just Putin, but Gorbachev, Yeltsin and Medvedev too. The Foreign Secretary, William Hague, was either becoming somewhat semi-detached or sensed that the German, French and Polish diplomatic efforts were already doomed. The UK seemed content to wait on the sidelines.

In the Ukraine Association Agreement, Article 4.1 contains the following words: 'Political dialogue of all areas of mutual interest shall be further developed and strengthened between the Parties. This will promote gradual convergence on foreign and security matters with the aim of Ukraine's ever deeper involvement into the European security area.' This was reiterated in Article 7.1, which called for convergence in foreign affairs, security and defence. Article 10.3 mentioned 'conflict prevention, crisis management and military-technological cooperation' and went on to state: 'The European Defence Agency [EDA] will establish close contact to discuss military capability improvement, including technological issues.'

In Moscow, not unreasonably from Putin's point of view, those words 'military capability' were seen as provocative. Putin's apprehension was now confirmed that the EU was mirroring NATO and was following in the path established first by President Clinton and then President George

W. Bush, set to ignore all the confidence-building assurances given to Gorbachev and Yeltsin by President Bush Sr that they would not take NATO up to every part of Russia's borders in Europe.

It should have been no surprise in Brussels by the end of 2013 that the democratically elected President Viktor Yanukovych, whose electoral strength lay in the Russian-speaking parts of Ukraine, was starting to shy away from the EU's Association Agreement. Why was he, as the elected President, apparently given no amelioration, no changes in wording? Or was he rejecting them? We need to know more about the line by line negotiations. Under pressure from Russia, Yanukovych tried to establish closer ties with the Russian Federation's plans for a trade and economic agreement with countries that had been formally in the Soviet sphere of influence. This was the more prudent alternative for him personally as well as for that part of Ukraine, in which he had electoral strength, where the people were more comfortable with Russia.

A wave of demonstration and civil unrest in Ukraine against President Yanukovych, called the 'Euromaidan' protests, then began to show the importance of the Agreement to the pro-European parts of the Ukraine; within them were some out-and-out nationalists, all sensing Yanukovych's change of attitude. These escalated in January 2014 when Yanukovych's government came forward with new anti-protest laws aimed at consolidating his grip on power. The violence and riots which followed, starting on 18 February, lead to 98 deaths and thousands injured.

What then happened was called EU diplomacy. But was it really? It consisted of the German, French and Polish Foreign

Ministers going to Kiev to negotiate with Yanukovych's government. Then the signing of a document on 21 February between Yanukovych and opposition leaders. The extent of the involvement of the CDSP and the External Affairs Secretariat is not yet very clear in this initiative but on 19 February the High Representative, then Catherine Ashton, did ask Sikorski, an inflammatory choice, to begin a diplomatic mission to Kiev. But on whose authority? Was it the Council of Ministers? The UK, a signatory to the 1994 Budapest Memorandum with Ukraine and the Russian Federation, was not represented. France who signed separately was represented, as was Germany. Was the UK deliberately omitted or did they not want to be involved? The US, another signatory to the Memorandum, were not formally involved but President Obama did speak to President Putin to press on him the need for a Russian presence and for a helpful Russian to join the diplomacy who could work with the EU negotiating team. The ink was barely dry on this so-called EU-brokered agreement when Yanukovych felt forced to flee from the capital and on 22 February 2014 members of parliament found him unable to fulfil his duties. The EU credibility and authority was openly shredded overnight. A body like the EU that claims great influence must not allow its own settlements to be disowned without a struggle to hold the two sides together. If it was not feasible it should not have been advocated and supported by the EU.

On the night of 22–23 February Putin discussed the extrication of the deposed President Yanukovych, who had become President after what observers considered a fairly-conducted election. Putin with his security team began the policy of returning Crimea to Russia. On 23 February pro-Russian demonstrations were held in the city of Sevastopol and by 27 February Russian troops without insignia took over the Supreme Council of Crimea. European and American sanctions against the annexation of Crimea followed and meanwhile fighting had started to break out in Eastern Ukraine.

Over time the fighting that erupted in Eastern Ukraine led to numerous high-profile diplomatic meetings and telephone calls involving President Putin, Chancellor Merkel and President Hollande amongst many other heads of government. Again it is not clear how much involvement came from the EU High Representative and officials from External Affairs. A potentially important agreement between the parties to the dispute was signed on 5 September 2014 but it proved useless. Merkel and Hollande met with Putin in Minsk on 11 February 2015 and a form of ceasefire was achieved. By the summer of 2015 a civil war was raging in the east, although the rest of Ukraine was peaceful if tense. Meanwhile, Putin was still riding high in the polls in Russia and though the economy was hurt by economic sanctions, the public was in no mood for a settlement, any more than the newly elected President of Ukraine, Petro Poroshenko, was able to persuade Ukrainians to compromise. His standing with his people was one of great weakness in relation to Putin's standing in Russia.

The shooting down of a civilian aircraft overflying Ukraine from Amsterdam to Kuala Lumpur on 17 July the previous year had for months shocked and soured the international atmosphere. The Dutch government, however, with many of their people killed, had wisely adopted a tough legal position and correctly wanted to be very clear on the evidence, some of which it made public in the summer of 2015. If, as some expect, the evidence still to be published points to the shooting down of the aircraft having been caused by pro-Russian separatists then the Netherlands are likely to take the whole issue to the International Court of Justice, which is empowered to award heavy damages as it did on the US over the Iranian plane which they mistakenly shot down. What was surprising in all this EU diplomacy was how little detailed follow-through there appeared to be. Proposals came eventually from the German side for a major devolution of power for Eastern Ukraine that Germany, with its own federal *Länder* system, was well equipped to provide. Yet the EU established no high-profile diplomatic mission to keep open a continuous dialogue with the combatants. It is hard to avoid concluding that by August 2015 the EU diplomatic effort appeared to have fizzled out.

Then, on 2 October, Putin met in Paris with Hollande and Merkel and there was some hopeful comment about the Ukraine. A few days later however, it emerged that Russia had begun flying military aircraft into Syria. Initially all Russian publicity was focused on their readiness to attack ISIL forces, but it soon became apparent their concern was that Assad's forces were losing ground to a mixture of forces. The preponderance of the Russian attacks were not on ISIL but designed to keep open vital road links between Damascus and the coast and to save Aleppo.

As someone who has long been arguing that ISIL posed a serious threat to Damascus, I thought criticism of Russian intervention was exaggerated and that Russia was acting militarily in the hope that they could also, when the immediate threat was over, play a major role in the negotiating process. This is exactly what happened when at long last all the related parties in the Middle East reassembled around the table in Vienna on 14 November 2015 with the vital addition of Iran, whose presence was accepted through gritted teeth by the Saudis.

The Syrian peace talks that are now underway will be very difficult. But it may be that Russia will take a more flexible position here and in negotiating a settlement in East Ukraine. There are many reasons for Russia giving the highest priority to diplomacy, not least the low oil price and the Western economic sanctions that are starting to do serious harm to the Russian economy. EU solidarity on these sanctions so far has held up, but again because sanctions are part of US, EU and NATO strategy they are far more likely to be adhered to than if the EU were acting alone.

Compressing such complex issues cannot do justice to the centuries of Russian–Ukrainian relations but two issues from the recent past must not be forgotten. The first is that the EU/Ukraine Agreement triggered the conflict in the Ukraine. The second is that the UK, with the US and Russia, signed in 1994 the Budapest Memorandum which was ignored by the annexation of Crimea. The signatories to that agreement reaffirmed 'their obligation to refrain from the threat or use of force against the territorial integrity or political independence of Ukraine'. Even as recently as 4 December 2009 the US and Russia confirmed these assurances and recorded them at a meeting. The memorandum had been issued from Budapest in order to help Ukrainian public opinion accept that more than

4,000 strategic and tactical nuclear weapons should be transferred from the Ukraine to Russia, in addition to 1,900 strategic nuclear warheads – a larger arsenal than Britain, France and China combined. Also included were 130 SS-19 ICBMs, 46 SS-24 ICBMs and 44 strategic bombers with hundreds of air-launched cruise missiles.[5] The annexation of Crimea will be cited by many sensible Ukrainians, and elsewhere in the world, for decades to come as the vindication for those who believe 'if you have nuclear weapons never give them up and if you have not got nuclear weapons find a way of getting some'.

It is, therefore, vital that the legal position of Crimea remains on the international agenda. There should be no formal recognition of Crimea being part of the Russian Federation, implicit or explicit, and instead a negotiated resolution must be sought, perhaps in the context of Transnistria being given up by the Russian Federation. Crimea's annexation is a test of international law as practised within the UN Charter. NATO action over Kosovo was the start of big countries like the US, UK and France – all permanent members of the Security Council – acting outside the UN Charter's formal wording. Crimea was the Russian reply. It is a fact that some EU countries still refuse to recognise the legal case for the humanitarian military intervention over Kosovo. Crimea's annexation will not be reversed, but it can and should be retrospectively settled within the UN Charter. The best forum for settling it is the P5+1 (Germany) forum used successfully in July 2015 after years of dialogue over the Iranian nuclear issue.

Why should Russia negotiate? There is one strong reason for doing so. Russia might be able to achieve by negotiation a UN-endorsed agreement where NATO and the EU recognise the prescient wisdom of the American diplomat George Kennan about NATO's boundaries. In an interview with Thomas L. Friedman of the *New York Times* on 2 May 1998, Kennan denounced the form of NATO expansion that had just been agreed by the US Senate:

> I think it is the beginning of a new Cold War. I think the Russians will gradually react quite adversely and it will affect their policies. I think it is a tragic mistake. There was no reason for this whatsoever. No one was threatening anybody else. This expansion would make the Founding Fathers of this country turn over in their graves. We have signed up to protect a whole series of countries, even though we have neither the resources nor the intention to do so in any serious way. [NATO expansion] was simply a lighthearted action by a Senate that has no real interest in foreign affairs.
>
> I was particularly bothered by the references to Russia as a country dying to attack Western Europe. Don't people understand? Our differences in the Cold War were with the Soviet Communist regime. And now we are turning our backs on the very people who mounted the greatest bloodless revolution in history to remove that Soviet regime.

Kennan has been proven right in every particular. A settlement of both Eastern Ukraine and Crimea could take years. Hopefully it will not, but to happen the P5+1 must agree terms of reference and decide whether to go wider than

Ukraine and include Georgia, Moldova and even Kosovo. It might make it easier for Russia to attend if the agenda went wider than Crimea.

There was an additional warning of how Russia was likely to act in Ukraine that stems from Georgia. In 2006 the US, the UK and most of NATO wanted to admit Georgia but Germany did not rally to a consensus, which is how NATO operates. Very wisely and courageously Chancellor Merkel blocked the initiative. Had she not done so in 2008, when Georgia was the scene of a direct military clash with Russian troops in 2010, NATO would have been obliged under Article 5 to defend Georgia though I suspect it would not have done so. President Medvedev was in charge of Russian foreign policy over Georgia while Putin was Prime Minister but heavily involved. Initially there was an attempt in some Western democracies to go along with the Georgian claim that they had been attacked by Russia, but this claim became ever harder to support. Later an official EU investigation concluded it was wrong.

In summary form there were two conclusions. Firstly, the Georgian President had ordered his forces to fire first; secondly, the Russians had made a disproportionate response when coming through the tunnel on 8 August from North Ossetia to South Ossetia where they remain today. They are also still in Abkhazia. Russia very quickly saw, indeed anticipated, that there was no readiness within NATO, even had Georgia been a member, to fulfil in the first few days the Article 5 guarantee to come in militarily in defence of Georgia's territorial integrity. The reason why that Article was very unlikely to have been invoked needs to be faced up to. It was not just because of concerns over who fired first, nor questions over the politically provocative stance of the then President of Georgia, who is now strangely the Governor of Odessa in Ukraine, but because of an innate sense within NATO governments that this was not a situation where public opinion would have supported war.

In truth, too, for much the same reasons, Article 5 would have been difficult to invoke if Ukraine had been in NATO in 2014 when Russia annexed Crimea. But it is essential Putin be convinced now, in 2016, that Article 5 would be invoked if any Baltic state were to be subjected to similar tactical military incursions as happened and are still happening in Ukraine. What is the problem over NATO's authority? Does it lie with the EU? Does it lie with NATO? Or is it, as I believe, a reflection of the dysfunctional relationship between the two organisations in terms of financial support and planning input? In Europe we are sleepwalking not just towards challenges in the Eurozone but to security problems because of EU competition with NATO; Prime Minister Cameron should recognise these issues have to feature in the negotiations before the referendum vote.

There is no shadow of doubt that after Ukraine all EU Member States who are also in NATO should increase their defence budgets to 2 per cent of their GDP, as agreed in the Wales summit of September 2014. Sadly, there is no chance that they all will, but at least the UK has committed itself in 2015 to do so. In future there must also be less talk about military matters in EU documents – such as the EU/Ukraine Agreement – less talk about EU common defence, and a greater commitment to NATO.

There is much confusion and ambiguity over 'common defence'. On 6 October 2000, Prime Minister Tony Blair went to Warsaw to make a much-heralded and, one has to presume, therefore calculated speech in which he called for the EU to become 'a superpower, but not a superstate'. With all allowances for the age of the sound bite these two words, 'superpower' and 'superstate', are inextricably linked and cannot simply be divorced from each other. It is impossible in the 21st century for an EU of 28 separate Member States to exercise 'superpower', as we have come to use that word, without the EU becoming a superstate. There have never been more than two global superpowers co-existing at any one time since the beginning of the 20th century. At the start of the century, there was Britain and Germany. After the First World War Britain and the US. From 1942 the USSR and US. Following the break-up of the Soviet Union in 1990 the US became the only superpower. Today, there are two superpowers again, namely the US and China. The term 'common defence' has its origin in the joint declaration signed in St Malo in December 1998 by Tony Blair and Jacques Chirac, saying that the European Union 'must have the capacity for autonomous action, backed up by credible military forces, the means to decide to use them, and a readiness to do so, in order to respond to international crises'. This shift in policy in St Malo has taxed British diplomatic skills, since it has become ever more obvious that France is operating from a different agenda and has different military aspirations. The then US Secretary of State, Madeleine Albright, responded for the Americans in a speech since referred to as the 'Three Ds', which called for the avoidance of 'de-coupling, duplication and discrimination' and said the US would examine any proposal on European defence and security with a simple question: Does it improve our effectiveness in working together? That question in 2016 remains unanswered. But it must be answered as part of any serious UK negotiation for a different relationship for a Non-Eurozone country not part of the Schengen area and fully committed to ensuring a continued major involvement of the US and Canada in NATO.

The military professionals on both sides of the Atlantic are virtually united in the need for NATO's planning role to maintain an overarching responsibility for the EU rapid reaction force, because this force cannot but affect NATO force levels, equipment and fighting potential. British military and intelligence officers felt very let down by their country's politicians pussyfooting around on this issue. The true picture was revealed by President Clinton's former head of the CIA, James Woolsey, speaking in Washington after the Nice negotiations and on its consequences: 'The one and only thing that the United States asked of our European friends was not to establish a separate and independent military planning capability. And, of course, that is precisely what they did.'[6] That quote encapsulates the key issue, which all NATO professionals fear has been conceded; meanwhile the true meaning of 'autonomy' when used by the French and some others in Europe for the ESDP and what has followed in CDSP is not just about deploying without American troops from NATO but doing so without American goodwill and even planning a deployment against the interests of the US. Some Europeans say this independence is necessary if the EU is not to be subservient to the US. If this is pursued it will be a certain recipe for the US to withdraw more forces from Europe, in the process turning NATO into a mere talking shop and effectively withdrawing any US responsibilities for common defence.

The European heads of government never learnt the lesson of Kosovo: airpower alone is not enough. The illusion of an EU ready to undertake common defence is reflected in the fact that the US is paying 75 per cent of the costs of NATO. The EU and NATO can credibly build up the more achievable part of the Cologne Declaration, namely 'the ability to take decisions on the full range of conflict prevention and crisis management tasks defined in the Treaty on European Union, the so-called "Petersberg tasks"'. Libya similarly showed that airpower is not enough but also that ground troops are needed in addition in considerable numbers. The same lesson comes from Afghanistan, Iraq and Syria. Over Libya, the no-fly zone and protection of civilians under the UN Security Council resolution allowed NATO to tilt the balance of fighting, but not to control the different rebel forces. What Kosovo showed conclusively, particularly after what had happened in the five wars that followed the break-up of the former Yugoslavia, was that a European Union defence force, relying on its own military capabilities and a diffuse leadership, without US backing, will not have the capacity to destroy air defences nor the political will to deploy sufficient troops.

Nevertheless, even with NATO the EU has taken a long time to resolve the problems bequeathed by the UN administration in both Bosnia-Herzegovina and Kosovo. A stable, secure and independent Bosnia and Kosovo cannot emerge with the sort of ethnic confrontation that we are seeing in Bosnia-Herzegovina and in parts of Macedonia. There has been a tendency for the US to pull back from the Balkans since the Dayton Agreement in 1995 and the EU and Russia wanted this to happen. But the lesson before and since Dayton is that more is achieved when the US and EU act together. NATO, after Afghanistan, Iraq, Libya and Syria, is no longer a purely Atlantic Alliance but a military grouping that can be utilised under the UN Charter; just as Russian forces were used by the UN in Bosnia-Herzegovina, one day China will also be used by the UN.

What the different wars in the former Yugoslavia all demonstrate is that even so-called EU 'Petersberg tasks' can be difficult to fulfil. This was re-emphasised by the reluctance of some NATO countries to deploy forces anywhere other than in Kabul following the initial defeat of the Taliban government in Afghanistan by American and the Northern Alliance forces in 2001–2. There are painful lessons that NATO peacekeepers have experienced in Afghanistan, particularly when they began to be regarded as an occupying force. NATO withdrawal before a US withdrawal became inevitable by 2014. For many involved it could not come too soon, but it was not a victory; as so often in the past, Afghanistan has proved the undoing of powerful invading forces.

If Europe pursues autonomous defence then we cannot expect US commitments to NATO to remain unchanged. The reality of the EU having said 'yes' to autonomy is that, from time to time, the EU will be contemplating force to support a foreign policy initiative where European interests and the American interests are opposed. We need to face these implications head on for they are profound and carry huge risks. Such a growing asymmetry in the transatlantic relationship was dealt with by Strobe Talbott, then US Deputy Secretary of State, when speaking in London in October 1999 about the need 'to rebalance our respective roles'. He went on to warn: 'We would not want to see an ESDI that comes into being first within NATO but then grows out of NATO and finally grows away from NATO, since that would lead to an ESDI that initially duplicates NATO but that could eventually compete with NATO.'

Talbott's word 'compete' is the nub of the issue over the present CSDP. His concerns were lost sight of after Iraq went wrong and when the US wanted to have the NATO support they refused immediately after 9/11. If CSDP continues to compete with the US it will lead to US withdrawal. EU–NATO competition, which under the direction of French pressure is becoming the European defence posture, will not be funded by the US Congress. The US will not stay around militarily in central Europe if competition becomes the hallmark of European defence. It may well keep bases in Turkey, and perhaps in Iceland, but it will distance itself from Eurozone defence pretensions. A lot will depend on German influence within a Eurozone. In Poland the new government has far less enthusiasm for Eurozone entry than the previous government. Will Germany resist French demands for more 'common defence' whilst simultaneously having to strain the France-German alliance by insisting that the French take tough disciplinary measures to make structural reforms to live with financial disciplines. I doubt it. Prior to the UK referendum, the UK must have a clear position agreed that we can withdraw from CSDP, and even CFSP, if its decision-making becomes more integrated and less consensual.

The European treaties already make detailed provision for cooperation in the area of defence and security, the most important of which is the 'permanent structured co-operation' in Articles 42 and 46 of the Lisbon Treaty. Also provision is made in Articles 42 and 45 for participation in projects within the framework of the European Defence Agency. Participation of groups of Member States in joint operations or tasks involving the use of civilian and military means is provided for in Article 44. This cooperation is open to Member States 'whose military capability fulfils higher criteria and which have made more binding commitments to one another in this area with a view to the most demanding missions'. The details of permanent structure cooperation are set out in a Protocol to the Lisbon Treaty. A Member State seeking to participate in permanent structured cooperation undertakes a number of obligations to develop its defence capacities and to participate in the main European equipment programmes and specifically in the activities of the European Defence Agency. It can be clearly seen therefore that the detailed structures for common defence are far advanced. It is only their implementation that has been held back, largely because of opposition from the UK and the fear of other Member States that to cross this divide might lead to a very serious pull-back of the United States from NATO. But an integrated Eurozone will be likely to cross that divide.

The US still wants to know if its EU allies are partially or fully committed to NATO's defence strategy. After the St Malo Agreement between President Chirac and Prime

Minister Blair, which first used the word 'autonomous', it was incumbent on the British to stand firm when the French, as they were bound to, tried to chip away at the centrality of NATO to any new design for European defence decision-making. The French were also bound to expand autonomy from meaning 'operating autonomously' to 'planning autonomously'. This is precisely what has happened and the French Chief of Defence Staff, in denying that there is an American right of first refusal, explicitly laid out the procedure on 28 March 2001: 'If the EU works properly, it will start working on crises at a very early stage, well before the situation escalates. NATO has nothing to do with this. At a certain stage the Europeans would decide to conduct a military operation. Either the Americans would come or not.' At one stage, before Nice, British officials tried to get the Dutch and the Germans to act for them in insisting on NATO planning being given the central position because they were so fearful of exposing Britain as having to veto the French position. Not unreasonably they refused and the French got exactly what they most wanted: prime responsibility for military planning and with it the freedom to plan autonomously. Nice could prove to be the most costly British diplomatic blunder since appeasement in the late 1930s. Some ground may have been won back since Nice as some issues were fudged and postponed. But I fear that Nice started a process whereby the US military, hitherto the most enthusiastic part of American policymakers for NATO, began disengaging from European defence.

The outgoing US Defence Secretary in the Clinton administration, himself a Republican, warned in December 2000 that NATO would become a 'relic' if the EU developed its own defence force. He was expressing a widespread concern in the Pentagon which preceded the arrival of George W. Bush. It was soon clear that Bush's new Secretary of Defence, Donald Rumsfeld, shared his predecessor's concerns. Returning to government service, having been ambassador to NATO under President Ford and the chairman of the bipartisan Congressional committee which had come out in favour of developing a missile defence system, Rumsfeld made it clear before February 2001 that he expected better of Britain than to acquiesce in the military documentation presented at Nice. As a new President, Bush avoided a confrontation but made his support conditional on Tony Blair's own assessment to him of what the Nice agreements meant. He quoted Blair's interpretation back publicly at their joint press conference at Camp David on 23 February 2001, saying, 'He also assured me that the European defence would no way undermine NATO. He also assured me that there would be a joint command, that planning would take place within NATO, and that should all NATO not wish to go on a mission, that would then serve as a catalyst for the [EU] defence forces moving on their own.' The problem was, as the defence specialists in the UK and US teams knew at Camp David, Blair's assurances were not an accurate interpretation of what had been agreed at Nice.

It is the envisaged size of the European rapid reaction force – 60,000–80,000 men, 300–350 fighter planes and 80 ships – that makes it obvious that if drawn from European countries contributing to NATO, something that has, as yet, not been achieved, it will create a considerable dent in NATO's earmarked force levels. There are still no concrete plans for the rapid reaction force to be additional to the force levels Europe has already promised to NATO. The rapid reaction force was to be deployable in theatre in sixty days and sustainable for a year. Typically, Europe has not met this optimistic target but nor has it met NATO targets. European NATO countries rarely fulfil their pledges on time to deploy forces. Few of their forces are equipped with intra-operable equipment, or are capable of matching in many respects the sophistication of their US partners. But still the pretension persists.

General Sir Rupert Smith, soon after retiring as Deputy SACEUR, with a distinguished career in Northern Ireland, the Gulf and the Balkans, said of any European rapid reaction force: 'at the higher end of the possible scenarios, or Petersberg task list, it must be able to fight as a force. This will require systems to fight the deep battle, that is to say long-range rocket and artillery weapons with the necessary target acquisition systems. In addition within this range of systems, we must also have an evident ability to escalate, to be more forceful because the initial application of forces is only fully credible if it is evidently backed by the means and will to see the job through despite enemy action and setbacks.'[7] It is impossible to see the development of such a capacity in a European rapid reaction force other than at the expense of NATO's capability.

The annexation of Crimea reminds us why the historic decision to form NATO was made after periodic US military involvement in Europe. The US military did not come in on the ground in the First World War until April 1918, but it still made a decisive difference to France and Britain's victory over Germany and Austria-Hungary. Only after Pearl Harbor was attacked by the Japanese in December 1941 could President Franklin Roosevelt, for all his strength domestically, overcome public resistance to being dragged in to another war in Europe. He declared war on Japan after Pearl Harbor, whereupon Germany declared war on the United States. A wiser and less hubristic man than Hitler[8] would have instead distanced Germany from Japan's 'day of infamy' and in so doing made it much harder for Roosevelt to come into the European War. President Truman only reversed his predecessor's decision to withdraw US troops made in 1945 when faced by the Soviet threat as it became recognised in the USA in 1946–7. It was a courageous reversal of America's traditional reluctance to station troops abroad when they signed up for NATO and agreed a continued military presence in Europe. It is not inevitable that they will stay. All US tanks have already gone from Europe.

In 2016, the Americans will still be ready to keep troops as allies on the ground in Europe, something they have done since 1943. But if the Eurozone integration leads to the French interpretation of autonomy it will not just be a US President, but senators and congressmen and the professional servicemen in the Pentagon, who will judge it incompatible with upholding their national interest for America to be retaining its troops on the ground in Europe.

In theory the European Union is a rich and powerful entity capable of developing its own military power. But it has chosen not to do so, and has not shaken off the mood of unilateral nuclear disarmament that swept the European continent in the 1970s and 1980s involving the Netherlands, Belgium, Scandinavia, and the socialist parties in Germany and Britain. To anyone who is not blinded by prejudice, Europe has needed over all these years the moorings of an Atlantic alliance. From many different perspectives European public opinion does not wish for the EU to seek superpower status. It makes no sense to champion a European military distinct from NATO. Let us not forget that the Italian and German governments called publicly for a bombing pause within days of NATO's air strikes commencing against Serbia over Kosovo. They were held to military action by the US, the UK and France. The majority of EU countries refused to be involved in the 1991 Gulf War, a war which was supported by the UN and involved Saddam Hussein invading Kuwait. Yet it must also be said that France and Germany opposed the 2003 Iraq War which was supported by the UK, Spain and Poland.

Within the EU there are few nations who wish, and are ready, to exercise power and support that exercise of power with military forces. The British and French can, and at times do, stiffen the EU to make it readier to exert diplomatic power and reinforce it with military power. Were an integrated Eurozone to develop in ways that stifled and reduced that sense of nationhood in both countries, Europe would be much weakened globally. But that combination, even when France and Britain are working well together, and joined by Germany and Italy, does not represent superpower. What Europe needs for its foreign and defence policies is realism and close cooperation between the EU and NATO.

Any such periods of military tension, let alone any new war in Europe, will not have the certainties of the Cold War in Europe because there are no longer such clear frontiers, nor is there the same clash of ideology with Soviet communism. Our situation is nearer that of the early part of the 20th Century with military challenges to the map of Europe, talk of encirclement and many uncertainties.[9] In this climate on 4 August 2015, Sergei Shoigu, the Defence Minister of the Russian Federation, announced a $60 billion reorganisation of its armed forces, focused on the S-400 surface-to-air missile with a range of 250 miles and the new S-500, designed to intercept intercontinental missiles, to defend Russia from the US and NATO. Russia is also taking significant steps to improve its navy.

All this demonstrates that in the light of the Budapest Memorandum the UK and the US must live up to their responsibilities and take an initiative for peace to settle disputed boundaries in Ukraine, Moldova and Georgia. They must involve Russia, France and China as permanent members of the Security Council, and Germany as the country already most heavily involved in the diplomacy of Ukraine. US and EU economic sanctions will have to stay in place, but even though they have had a serious effect on the Russian economy they have had no obvious effect yet on its policy towards Eastern Ukraine and will not of themselves change anything over Crimea. The model for any such negotiation, as already stated, is the successfully concluded Iran Agreement, though the Russians will not dream of participating in an E3+P3 format. EU involvement, though it worked well over Iran at first, only stemmed from the initial refusal of the US to get involved at all. Over these European boundary disputes, as in the later stages of the Iran negotiations, the US will have a key role to play because their financial sanctions are the ones Russia needs removing. Russia already blames EU involvement for the situation in Ukraine. The incentive for Russian participation must be explicit wording in the terms of reference that one of the aims of the initiative is the mutual recognition, on successful completion of the negotiation, of the definition of the boundaries of the Russian Federation with those of NATO countries, coupled with the military operations of any EU Common Security and Defence Policy. The essentials for Ukraine in participating are that they settle for boundaries that do not seek to maximise its territory but are instead historically and militarily defensible. Looking to the future, Ukraine can remove as much as possible of the poisoned atmosphere, demonstrate beyond a narrow definition that their people wish to live in their territory, and by agreement become part of the EEA Single Market.

The Turkish election result of November 2015 is a clear indication that there is a majority in Turkey ready to live with the authoritarianism which Erdoğan's critics complain about. Yet, in fairness to Erdoğan, much of the criticism outside the country started before his authoritarianism had manifested itself and continues to this day. It stems from his much earlier refusal to give permission to US and UK forces in 2003, just after he and the AKP came to power, to attack Iraq from Turkish territory. The harsh truth is that Erdoğan was right to spot the flaws in Bush and Blair's thinking. He was also right to switch out of his previous close relationship with President Assad of Syria; had NATO followed his advice and given its support to the moderate Syrian military opposition it is possible that the long, tragic, horrendous civil war in that country could have been avoided and Assad removed, especially if the views of the then British Chief of Defence Staff, General Richards, had been accepted and tens of thousands of Syrians had been extracted from the country and then trained in bordering countries.[10] Five years later we are at last negotiating a Syrian settlement and Assad's position is being represented, in part, by Russia and Iran. Negotiations are a welcome change.

The year 2016 should be the moment for the EU to take an initiative with Turkey, as argued at the beginning of the this booklet, and reinforce its friendship by negotiating a place for Turkey as a full voting member in the Single Market EEA. But already the critics are citing, as a means of discouragement, that the Turkish military are attacking Kurdish fighters inside Turkey and on its borders. These concerns are legitimate but they should not be used to block this EEA initiative, for other EU Member States over the years have had to grapple with militant separatism. The Kurdish problem is longstanding; it will not be settled easily or quickly.

Bluntly, there is, after the Turkish elections of 2015, a choice – NATO and the EU should embark on a more positive approach to Turkey, not just to help with migration to Europe from Syria, but to influence Turkish policy in the whole Middle East region. Through extending the hand of friendship they would contribute to the restructuring of a wider Europe through the EEA and thereafter give Serbia an early incentive to help keep Bosnia-Herzegovina united. Joining the EEA now would not slow the Serbian path to EU membership any more than it is being slowed already by general reluctance of the Member States to enlarge at all.

Standing aside and letting Turkey, a large democratic Muslim state, drift away from the EU and NATO would be a tragic loss of opportunity – Turkey has so much to contribute, not least in dealing with ISIL. The EU has already been urging three predominantly Muslim countries to work towards membership – Bosnia-Herzegovina, Albania and Kosovo – but they, too, could be better to start with EEA membership before EU membership. There are, as we know, large Muslim communities within many existing EU countries. Centuries ago, in Spain, it became evident that Muslims would play an important role in Europe's development and a purely Christian Europe has never been a credible proposition. Turkey wants and deserves to be treated with respect, and have a position in European decision-making consistent with its position in G20.

Protests in Syria began in March 2011 and developed into a civil war. The case for intervention from outside was redolent with memories of Libya and bedevilled by the number of separate Sunni military forces, some of whom it was very hard to justify giving weapons to. It had also been known for some time that the more acceptable elements to whom one could have supplied arms had links with more undesirable elements like ISIL, then strengthening in Iraq. With arms passing to and fro the consequences of bombing just for retaliation purposes in 2013 was very hard to justify.

If President Obama had gone ahead with the planned limited bombing on Assad in late August 2013, I am convinced that it would then have been held responsible, albeit unfairly, for reviving ISIL, which lead in June 2014 to massive world news headlines about them taking Mosul in Iraq and capturing US weaponry in large numbers. This action also helped to build up ISIL strength to take Palmyra in Syria in 2015. Abu

Musab al-Zarqwi, the founder of the Islamic State, began to build his insurgency operation in Iraq in 2003; though he was killed in 2006 by a US air strike, by the time the US had pulled out in 2011 the Islamic State under its new leader, Abu Bakr al-Baghdadi, was starting to expand into Syria and build up in Iraq. All this was known in 2013. It was not foolish to make a distinction between Iraq, where British forces were invited by the recognised government to help, and Syria where any action was not lawful in terms of UN Security Council authority. A far better course was the one which followed the losing of the House of Commons vote to negotiate away all chemical weapons, as I had argued for. In the event the UN did authorise chemical weapons to be taken out of Syria as was made possible under an initial Russian/American agreement. Deplorably, despite this, Assad used chlorine, not as lethal as sarin gas, and Russia should have called Assad to account. Yet Russia, after bombing in Syria, was to face retaliation by an IS section based in the Sinai putting a bomb on a Russian civilian plane flying from Sharm-El-Sheik to St Petersburg.

At the end of 2015 we are still underestimating the so-called ISIL forces in Syria in a suburb of Damascus. We are also forgetting that Russia's involvement in Syria is longstanding having had, as already explained, a deep water naval base in Tartus, from which they have operated since 1971. The Shi'ite Hezbollah fighting around Lebanon, long supported by Iran, also have good military reasons for encouraging Iran to increase military support in Syria and Iran has sent in ground troops. What is deeply distressing is our cuts to food budgets for UN agencies in camps in Syria, Lebanon and Jordan and how little many EU countries are contributing.

There is a warning to David Cameron and Jeremy Corbyn in these events that they should both remember. It is very dangerous to bring partisan domestic politics into the conduct of international affairs. Bipartisanship, wherever possible, is highly desirable. John Major, in 1991, on the eve of the first Iraq War to liberate Kuwait, decided not to exploit differences in the Labour Party even to the extent of avoiding calling a vote which would have been overwhelmingly supported in the House of Commons because he knew it would have created difficulties for Neil Kinnock, as Opposition leader, when a number of Labour MPs would have voted against.

The Middle East has had enough invasions, interventions and bombing. It needs now – and the sooner the better – a Middle East peace settlement. As the first step, such a regional settlement may require Syria to exist for some length of time with four semi-autonomous areas all helping to constrain and eventually defeat ISIL.[11] In all the years following the Arab Spring revolution starting in Tunisia in 2010, with the tragic turn of events in Egypt, it is hard to conclude that the EU's CFSP has had much influence except in Tunisia, let alone its CSDP, which has had virtually no influence militarily.

The UK referendum cannot escape being, in part, about EU defence policies and aspirations. This would be the case regardless, but it is increasingly important now that Jeremy Corbyn has been elected by a big majority of members and supporters as the leader of the Labour Party in Opposition. Labour, we are told, will recommend remaining in the EU. But what sort of EU does its leader want? What relationship, if any, between the EU and NATO?

I have always seen NATO as essential. As Foreign Secretary I opposed, and still oppose, Trident as an expensive financial inroad into our conventional defence effort. For the future, supersonic cruise missiles conventionally armed, but capable of carrying nuclear weapons at times of global tension, I see as a potentially cheaper and more prudent insurance policy for a UK hard pressed to fund two new large aircraft carriers.[12]

As to Jeremy Corbyn not wishing to personally authorise a nuclear response, Labour has already grappled with this issue in relation to Michael Foot. But he was not a pacifist. From 1974–79 Foot was, while a full member of the Defence and Overseas Cabinet Sub-Committee, never involved with four other Cabinet colleagues in nuclear discussions or nuclear implementation. During the General Election of 1983 the BBC captured the essence of the campaign by asking the three party leaders, 'Would you push the nuclear button?' Roy Jenkins prevaricated: 'I find it difficult to believe the situation would arise.' Michael Foot was obdurate: 'It would be utter criminal insanity for anyone to say they would press the button.' Margaret Thatcher considered the alternative: 'If we don't say we will press the button the Russians would sweep over Europe and us with conventional forces.' In all the hours of debate, those words on this crucial defence issue clarified the attitudes of the parties more than anything else.

At a later stage in the 1983 General Election in Bristol, I attacked Michael Foot's position revealing that the potential Prime Minister had deliberately avoided sharing responsibility on nuclear questions when in government and was not fit to govern in a possible few days time without telling us how he personally intended to handle this vital issue. Jeremy

Corbyn, to his credit, seems determined to face the issue from the start of his Labour leadership and is being far more straightforward and determined that Britain, under the Non-Proliferation Treaty, should fulfill its commitment to phase out, with other nuclear weapon states, all nuclear weapons. Despite much talk, excuses are constantly found for keeping, not reducing, our nuclear UK deterrent.

Any new leader of a political party is wise to adjust to their new responsibilities and reconsider past personal positions and Labour can use a few years thinking space to adjust and develop new defence and disarmament policies. It is an illusion, however, to believe that in the UK referendum on the EU these defence issues can simply be evaded. There are people in the UK who take a largely French view that Europe alone can deal with its own defence, that we do not need the US and need not worry about a decline in NATO. The facts simply do not bear this out in terms of the money EU countries spend, the numbers in the military and the quality and total armaments held. Yet NATO is more than the US. The newly-elected Canadian Prime Minister Trudeau warned President Obama of his election promise to end Canada's participation in airstrikes in Syria and Iraq, but that was before ISIL attacked Paris and may be made dependent on the result of negotiations.

It is not just Labour but Conservative MPs who have expressed reservations about military action in Syria without UN authority. The challenge is to use the NATO/Russian Council acting under the authority of the UN Security Council.

Corbyn may succeed, as a result of a Conference decision, in committing Labour to give up all nuclear weapons. This was debated and rejected when Bevan and Gaitskell combined together in 1957 and Bevan warned against going into an international conference chamber 'naked'. Then for a year between 1960–1961 the Labour Party Conference endorsed unilateralism. But Gaitskell fought and reversed that policy in a famous speech. Labour adopted unilateralism again in 1980 under Michael Foot. That became an SDP moment when it was accompanied by a commitment to come out of the European Community without even a referendum, which Labour had given in 1975, and also introducing the trade union block vote which ensured these two policies formed part of the Labour manifesto for the 1983 General Election. This was lost by a huge margin. Both policies were eventually abandoned by 1988–9.

Stopping all Trident submarine patrols from 2020 is certainly open to Labour if they win the 2020 General Election and senior defence officers can either resign or comply. A wiser path would be for Labour to focus on taking significant steps down the scale towards phasing out all nuclear weapons, as under the NPT, while meanwhile retaining a minimum deterrent. Corbyn shows little sign of wanting this option. In my judgement, if this option is rejected and accompanied by disdain or hostility to NATO it will be an SDP moment, or his party will remove him as leader which is what Labour did to its pacifist leader, Lansbury, in 1935.

Corbyn can try, if he wishes, to resolve his personal dilemma by delegating the nuclear decision to Cabinet colleagues. Some will argue that delegation is unacceptable in principle. Yet post the Iraq War debacle the Prime Minister's prerogative to declare war has been rightly circumscribed and Parliament, in all but a dire emergency, has to be involved in any decision. The British people are probably more ready, therefore, to accept someone as Prime Minister who openly declares the nuclear decision as a matter of conscience, and though he would be ready to preside over any collective meeting he would not vote. This is a very big political adjustment for the British electorate to make, particularly so for the older generation. In my view voters will only contemplate it if Corbyn proves a successful leader on domestic issues. The press thrive on the model of a decisive leader taking the key decisions. Unfortunately, they do not give much credence to the proven British Cabinet model of collective responsibility which served us so well from 1940 under the coalition War Cabinet.

Much has been written, and will continue to be written, that attempts to encapsulate the essence of America and the EU as they are today. The astringent comments of Robert Skidelsky, the biographer of Keynes, are worth repeating on why 'Robert Kagan's 2003 neo-conservative proposition, Americans are from Mars, Europeans from Venus, offered such a misleading guide. True enough, the European Union has gone farther down the pacifist road than the US. It is the weak nerve center of a flabby semi-state, with almost defenseless frontiers, where humanitarian rhetoric masks spinelessness. But America's sporadic, erratic, and largely ineffective deployment of power is hardly of Martian quality.'[13]

Every UK voter will have to examine what sort of country they wish to live in during this forthcoming referendum. It will not just mean restructuring to establish a new category of Non-Eurozone Member States, but also reform of existing methods of deciding EU foreign and defence policies.

Notes

This booklet has been drawn from Lord Owen's Inaugural Peter Hennessy Lecture at QMUL on 8 October 2015 and from his Introduction in his revised ebook edition of *Europe Restructured: The Eurozone Crisis and the UK Referendum* (London: Methuen, September 2014).

1. With the entry into force of the Lisbon Treaty, the EU's European Security and Defence Policy (ESDP) was re-baptised the Common Security and Defence Policy (CSDP). The Treaty also introduced a new mechanism for capability development, Permanent Structured Cooperation, which allows those Member States that are willing to enhance military integration between themselves within the framework of the EU. The CSDP has become a significant part of the Common Foreign and Security Policy (CFSP) following the dissolution of the Western European Union (WEU).

2. David Owen, *Europe Restructured. The Eurozone Crisis and the UK Referendum* (London: Methuen, 2014 ebook version).

3. David Richards, *Taking Command* (Headline, 2014) pp. 313–320.

4.   Stefan Auer, 'Carl Schmitt in the Kremlin: The Ukraine crisis and the return of geopolitics', *International Affairs:* 91:5 (2015) p. 956–7.

5.   David S. Yost, 'The Budapest Memorandum and Russia's intervention in Ukraine', *International Affairs: 91:3 (2015), pp. 505–38.*

6.   David Owen, *Balkan Odyssey* (Victor Gollanz, 1995) pp. 102–3, 136.

7.   General Sir Rupert Smith, 'The Development of a European Rapid Reaction Force', One World Trust, 29 November 2001.

8.   David Owen, *In Sickness and In Power. Illness in Heads of Government during the last 100 years,* rev. ed. (London: Methuen, 2011), pp. 27–37.

9.   David Owen, *The Hidden Perspective. The Military Conversations 1906–1914* (London: Haus Publishing, 2014).

10. David Richards, *Taking Command* (Headline, 2014) pp. 321.

11. David Owen, Letter, *The Times*, 17 November 2015.

12. David Owen, 'Reshaping the British Nuclear Deterrent', COMEC Occasional Paper No 5, 17 March 2015. http://www.comec.org.uk/publications/occasional.

13. Robert Skidelsky, 'Is western civilisation in terminal decline?', *Guardian*, 17 November 2015.